50 The Best Tea-Time Recipes

By: Kelly Johnson

Table of Contents

- Scones
- Lemon Drizzle Cake
- Victoria Sponge
- Earl Grey Shortbread
- Cucumber Sandwiches
- Clotted Cream and Jam Scones
- Tea Cakes
- Madeleines
- Fruit Tarts
- Blueberry Muffins
- Banana Bread
- Carrot Cake
- Mini Quiches
- Chocolate Eclairs
- Macarons
- Pistachio Biscotti
- Almond Cake

- Cheese Scones
- Pecan Pie Bars
- Cherry Bakewell Tarts
- Fig and Honey Scones
- Lavender Cookies
- Matcha Pound Cake
- Apple Crumble Bars
- Raspberry Thumbprint Cookies
- Vanilla Madeleines
- Lemon Bars
- Cinnamon Rolls
- Mini Victoria Sponges
- Chocolate Chip Scones
- Peanut Butter Cookies
- Apricot Danish
- Savory Puff Pastry Twists
- Lemon Poppy Seed Muffins
- Strawberry Shortcake
- Coconut Macaroons

- Mini Cheesecakes
- Date and Walnut Cake
- Chocolate Truffles
- Tea-Infused Ice Cream
- Savory Herb Scones
- Orange Loaf Cake
- Walnut Brownies
- Almond Florentines
- Chai Spiced Cookies
- Brie and Cranberry Tartlets
- Honey and Oat Bars
- Pumpkin Muffins
- Rhubarb Crumble
- Salted Caramel Brownies

Scones

Ingredients:

- 2 cups (250g) all-purpose flour
- 1/4 cup (50g) granulated sugar
- 1 tablespoon baking powder
- 1/2 teaspoon salt
- 1/2 cup (115g) cold unsalted butter, cut into cubes
- 2/3 cup (160ml) milk
- 1 teaspoon vanilla extract
- 1 egg, beaten (for brushing)

Instructions:

1. Preheat the oven to 400°F (200°C). Line a baking tray with parchment paper.
2. In a large bowl, whisk together the flour, sugar, baking powder, and salt.
3. Cut in the cold butter with a pastry cutter or fingertips until the mixture looks like breadcrumbs.
4. Stir in the milk and vanilla gently until just combined — do not overmix.
5. Turn the dough onto a floured surface, pat it into a 1-inch thick round, and cut out circles with a floured cutter.
6. Place scones on the tray, brush tops with beaten egg.
7. Bake for 12–15 minutes, until golden brown. Cool on a wire rack.

Lemon Drizzle Cake

Ingredients:

- 1/2 cup (115g) unsalted butter, softened
- 1 cup (200g) granulated sugar
- 2 large eggs
- 1 1/2 cups (190g) self-raising flour
- Zest of 2 lemons
- 1/2 cup (120ml) milk

For the drizzle:

- Juice of 2 lemons
- 1/3 cup (65g) granulated sugar

Instructions:

1. Preheat the oven to 350°F (175°C). Grease and line a loaf pan.
2. Beat together the butter and sugar until light and fluffy.
3. Add the eggs one at a time, mixing well after each.
4. Fold in the flour and lemon zest, then gradually mix in the milk.
5. Pour into the prepared pan and bake for 45–50 minutes, or until a skewer comes out clean.
6. While still warm, poke holes all over the cake with a skewer and pour over the lemon drizzle. Let it cool completely before slicing.

Victoria Sponge

Ingredients:

- 1 cup (225g) unsalted butter, softened
- 1 cup (225g) granulated sugar
- 4 large eggs
- 1 1/4 cups (225g) self-raising flour
- 2 tablespoons milk
- 1 teaspoon vanilla extract

For the filling:

- 1/2 cup (120ml) whipped cream or buttercream
- 1/4 cup (80g) raspberry jam
- Powdered sugar, for dusting

Instructions:

1. Preheat the oven to 350°F (175°C). Grease and line two 8-inch round cake tins.
2. Cream together the butter and sugar until pale and fluffy.
3. Beat in the eggs one at a time, adding a spoonful of flour with each to prevent curdling.
4. Gently fold in the remaining flour, milk, and vanilla until just combined.
5. Divide evenly between the two tins and bake for 20–25 minutes until golden and springy.

6. Cool completely, then spread jam on one cake layer, top with cream, and sandwich the second layer on top.

7. Dust with powdered sugar before serving.

Earl Grey Shortbread

Ingredients:

- 1 cup (225g) unsalted butter, softened
- 1/2 cup (100g) granulated sugar
- 2 cups (250g) all-purpose flour
- 2 tablespoons finely ground Earl Grey tea leaves
- 1/2 teaspoon salt

Instructions:

1. Preheat the oven to 325°F (160°C). Line a baking tray with parchment paper.
2. In a large bowl, beat together the butter and sugar until light and fluffy.
3. Add the flour, tea leaves, and salt, mixing until a dough forms.
4. Roll out the dough on a lightly floured surface to about 1/4-inch thickness.
5. Cut into desired shapes and place on the baking tray.
6. Bake for 12–15 minutes, until just lightly golden at the edges.
7. Cool on a wire rack before serving.

Cucumber Sandwiches

Ingredients:

- 1 cucumber, thinly sliced
- 1/2 cup (120g) cream cheese, softened
- 2 tablespoons fresh dill, chopped
- 1 tablespoon lemon juice
- Salt and pepper, to taste
- Thin white or whole wheat sandwich bread, crusts removed

Instructions:

1. In a bowl, mix the cream cheese, dill, lemon juice, salt, and pepper until smooth.
2. Spread a thin layer of the mixture onto each slice of bread.
3. Lay cucumber slices evenly over half of the bread slices.
4. Top with the remaining bread and gently press together.
5. Cut into fingers or triangles to serve.

Clotted Cream and Jam Scones

Ingredients:

- 2 cups (250g) self-raising flour
- 1/4 cup (50g) granulated sugar
- 1/2 teaspoon salt
- 1/2 cup (115g) unsalted butter, cold and cubed
- 2/3 cup (160ml) milk
- 1 teaspoon vanilla extract
- Clotted cream and strawberry jam, for serving

Instructions:

1. Preheat the oven to 400°F (200°C). Line a baking tray with parchment paper.
2. Mix the flour, sugar, and salt in a bowl.
3. Rub in the butter until the mixture resembles fine breadcrumbs.
4. Stir in the milk and vanilla until just combined.
5. Roll out gently and cut into rounds.
6. Bake for 12–15 minutes until golden.
7. Serve warm with generous spoonfuls of clotted cream and jam.

Tea Cakes

Ingredients:

- 2 1/2 cups (315g) all-purpose flour
- 1/4 cup (50g) granulated sugar
- 2 teaspoons instant yeast
- 1/2 teaspoon salt
- 1/2 teaspoon ground cinnamon
- 3/4 cup (180ml) warm milk
- 1 large egg
- 1/4 cup (55g) butter, softened
- 1/2 cup (75g) currants or raisins

Instructions:

1. In a large bowl, combine flour, sugar, yeast, salt, and cinnamon.
2. Add warm milk, egg, and butter, mixing to form a soft dough.
3. Knead until smooth, then work in the currants.
4. Cover and let rise until doubled, about 1 hour.
5. Shape into small rounds and place on a lined tray.
6. Let rise again for 30 minutes, then bake at 375°F (190°C) for 15–18 minutes.
7. Serve slightly warm with butter.

Madeleines

Ingredients:

- 2/3 cup (85g) all-purpose flour
- 3/4 teaspoon baking powder
- 1/2 cup (100g) granulated sugar
- 2 large eggs
- 1 teaspoon vanilla extract
- Zest of 1 lemon
- 1/2 cup (115g) unsalted butter, melted and cooled

Instructions:

1. Whisk the eggs and sugar until thick and pale.
2. Add vanilla and lemon zest.
3. Sift in the flour and baking powder, folding gently.
4. Fold in the melted butter carefully.
5. Chill the batter for 1 hour.
6. Preheat oven to 375°F (190°C). Grease a madeleine pan.
7. Spoon batter into molds, bake for 8–10 minutes until puffed and golden.
8. Dust with powdered sugar if desired.

Fruit Tarts

Ingredients:

- 1 sheet shortcrust pastry
- 1 cup (240ml) pastry cream
- Assorted fresh fruits (berries, kiwi, mango, etc.)
- 2 tablespoons apricot jam, warmed

Instructions:

1. Preheat the oven to 375°F (190°C). Line small tart tins with pastry and prick the bases.
2. Bake blind for 10–12 minutes until golden. Cool completely.
3. Fill each tart with pastry cream.
4. Arrange fresh fruit decoratively on top.
5. Brush lightly with warmed apricot jam for a glossy finish.

Blueberry Muffins

Ingredients:

- 2 cups (250g) all-purpose flour
- 1/2 cup (100g) granulated sugar
- 2 teaspoons baking powder
- 1/2 teaspoon baking soda
- 1/2 teaspoon salt
- 1 cup (240ml) buttermilk
- 1/3 cup (80ml) vegetable oil
- 1 large egg
- 1 teaspoon vanilla extract
- 1 cup (150g) fresh or frozen blueberries

Instructions:

1. Preheat the oven to 375°F (190°C). Line a muffin tin.
2. In one bowl, mix dry ingredients; in another, whisk wet ingredients.
3. Combine gently, then fold in blueberries.
4. Divide into muffin cups and bake for 18–22 minutes until golden.

Banana Bread
Ingredients:

- 2–3 ripe bananas, mashed
- 1/2 cup (115g) unsalted butter, melted
- 1 cup (200g) granulated sugar
- 1 large egg
- 1 teaspoon vanilla extract
- 1 1/2 cups (190g) all-purpose flour
- 1 teaspoon baking soda
- 1/2 teaspoon salt

Instructions:

1. Preheat the oven to 350°F (175°C). Grease a loaf pan.
2. Mix bananas with melted butter.
3. Stir in sugar, egg, and vanilla.
4. Add flour, baking soda, and salt, mixing just until combined.
5. Pour into the pan and bake for 50–60 minutes. Cool before slicing.

Carrot Cake
Ingredients:

- 2 cups (250g) all-purpose flour
- 2 teaspoons baking powder
- 1 teaspoon baking soda
- 1 1/2 teaspoons cinnamon
- 1/2 teaspoon nutmeg
- 1/2 teaspoon salt
- 1 cup (200g) granulated sugar
- 1/2 cup (100g) brown sugar
- 1 cup (240ml) vegetable oil
- 4 large eggs
- 2 cups (200g) finely grated carrots

For the frosting:

- 8oz (225g) cream cheese, softened
- 1/4 cup (60g) butter, softened
- 1 1/2 cups (180g) powdered sugar
- 1 teaspoon vanilla extract

Instructions:

1. Preheat the oven to 350°F (175°C). Grease and line two 8-inch cake pans.

2. Mix dry ingredients together.

3. In another bowl, beat sugars, oil, and eggs until smooth.

4. Stir in the dry ingredients, then fold in carrots.

5. Divide batter and bake for 25–30 minutes.

6. Cool, then sandwich and top with cream cheese frosting.

Mini Quiches

Ingredients:

- 1 sheet puff pastry
- 4 large eggs
- 1/2 cup (120ml) milk or cream
- 1/2 cup (60g) grated cheese
- 1/4 cup (40g) cooked bacon bits or vegetables
- Salt and pepper, to taste

Instructions:

1. Preheat the oven to 375°F (190°C). Grease a mini muffin tin.
2. Cut puff pastry into small rounds and line the tin.
3. Whisk eggs, milk, salt, and pepper together.
4. Fill each pastry shell with a bit of cheese, bacon, and egg mixture.
5. Bake for 15–18 minutes until puffed and golden.

Chocolate Eclairs

Ingredients:

- 1/2 cup (120ml) water
- 1/4 cup (60g) unsalted butter
- 1/2 cup (65g) all-purpose flour
- 2 large eggs
- 1 cup (240ml) whipped cream or pastry cream, for filling

For the chocolate glaze:

- 1/2 cup (85g) dark chocolate, melted
- 2 tablespoons heavy cream

Instructions:

1. Preheat the oven to 400°F (200°C). Line a baking sheet.
2. Heat water and butter until boiling, then stir in flour quickly.
3. Beat until the dough forms a ball; cool slightly.
4. Beat in eggs one at a time until smooth.
5. Pipe into 3-inch strips and bake for 20–25 minutes.
6. Cool, then split and fill with cream.
7. Mix chocolate and cream for glaze, then spread over the tops.

Macarons

Ingredients:

- 1 cup (100g) almond flour
- 1 3/4 cups (200g) powdered sugar
- 3 large egg whites, room temperature
- 1/4 cup (50g) granulated sugar
- Food coloring (optional)
- Filling of choice (buttercream, ganache, jam)

Instructions:

1. Sift almond flour and powdered sugar together.
2. Whisk egg whites until foamy, then gradually add granulated sugar until stiff peaks form.
3. Fold dry ingredients into the meringue carefully.
4. Add food coloring if desired.
5. Pipe small circles onto lined baking sheets.
6. Tap trays to release air bubbles and let sit for 30–60 minutes until a skin forms.
7. Bake at 300°F (150°C) for 15–18 minutes. Cool, then sandwich with filling.

Pistachio Biscotti

Ingredients:

- 1 3/4 cups (220g) all-purpose flour
- 1 teaspoon baking powder
- 1/4 teaspoon salt
- 1/2 cup (100g) granulated sugar
- 2 large eggs
- 1 teaspoon vanilla extract
- 3/4 cup (90g) shelled pistachios, roughly chopped

Instructions:

1. Preheat the oven to 350°F (175°C). Line a baking tray.
2. Mix flour, baking powder, salt, and sugar.
3. Beat eggs and vanilla, then mix into the dry ingredients.
4. Fold in pistachios.
5. Shape into a log and bake for 25 minutes.
6. Cool slightly, slice, and bake slices for 10–12 minutes per side until crisp.

Almond Cake

Ingredients:

- 1 cup (225g) unsalted butter, softened
- 1 cup (200g) granulated sugar
- 4 large eggs
- 1 teaspoon almond extract
- 1 1/4 cups (150g) all-purpose flour
- 1/2 cup (50g) ground almonds
- 1 1/2 teaspoons baking powder
- Powdered sugar, for dusting

Instructions:

1. Preheat the oven to 350°F (175°C). Grease a round cake tin.
2. Beat butter and sugar until fluffy.
3. Add eggs one at a time, then almond extract.
4. Fold in flour, ground almonds, and baking powder.
5. Pour into the tin and bake for 30–35 minutes.
6. Cool and dust with powdered sugar.

Cheese Scones

Ingredients:

- 2 cups (250g) all-purpose flour
- 1 tablespoon baking powder
- 1/2 teaspoon salt
- 1/4 teaspoon pepper
- 1/4 cup (60g) unsalted butter, cold and cubed
- 3/4 cup (90g) grated sharp cheddar cheese
- 2/3 cup (160ml) milk

Instructions:

1. Preheat the oven to 400°F (200°C). Line a baking tray.
2. Mix flour, baking powder, salt, and pepper.
3. Cut in butter until crumbly.
4. Stir in cheese, then milk to form a soft dough.
5. Roll out, cut into rounds, and bake for 12–15 minutes until golden.

Pecan Pie Bars
Ingredients:
For the crust:

- 1 1/2 cups (190g) all-purpose flour
- 1/2 cup (100g) granulated sugar
- 1/2 cup (115g) butter, softened

For the topping:

- 3 large eggs
- 3/4 cup (150g) brown sugar
- 1/2 cup (120ml) corn syrup
- 2 tablespoons melted butter
- 1 teaspoon vanilla extract
- 1 1/2 cups (150g) chopped pecans

Instructions:

1. Preheat the oven to 350°F (175°C). Grease a 9x13-inch pan.
2. Mix crust ingredients, press into pan, and bake for 20 minutes.
3. Whisk topping ingredients and pour over hot crust.
4. Bake another 25–30 minutes. Cool completely before cutting into bars.

Cherry Bakewell Tarts

Ingredients:

- 1 sheet shortcrust pastry
- 1/3 cup (100g) cherry jam
- 1/2 cup (60g) ground almonds
- 1/4 cup (50g) granulated sugar
- 1/4 cup (55g) butter, softened
- 1 large egg
- 1/2 teaspoon almond extract
- Powdered sugar, for icing

Instructions:

1. Preheat oven to 350°F (175°C). Line tart tins with pastry.
2. Spread a layer of jam in the bottom.
3. Cream butter, sugar, egg, ground almonds, and almond extract.
4. Spoon almond mixture over the jam.
5. Bake for 20–25 minutes. Cool, then drizzle with a simple powdered sugar glaze.

Fig and Honey Scones
 Ingredients:

- 2 cups (250g) all-purpose flour
- 1 tablespoon baking powder
- 1/4 teaspoon salt
- 1/4 cup (60g) cold unsalted butter, cubed
- 1/2 cup (75g) chopped dried figs
- 2 tablespoons honey
- 2/3 cup (160ml) milk

Instructions:

1. Preheat oven to 400°F (200°C). Line a baking tray.
2. Mix flour, baking powder, and salt.
3. Rub in butter until crumbly.
4. Stir in figs, honey, and milk until just combined.
5. Shape dough, cut into rounds, and bake for 12–15 minutes.

Lavender Cookies

Ingredients:

- 1/2 cup (115g) unsalted butter, softened
- 1/2 cup (100g) granulated sugar
- 1 large egg
- 1 teaspoon vanilla extract
- 1 1/2 cups (190g) all-purpose flour
- 1 teaspoon culinary lavender buds, finely chopped
- 1/2 teaspoon baking powder
- 1/4 teaspoon salt

Instructions:

1. Preheat oven to 350°F (175°C). Line a baking sheet.
2. Cream butter and sugar together.
3. Beat in egg and vanilla.
4. Stir in flour, lavender, baking powder, and salt.
5. Roll into small balls and flatten slightly.
6. Bake for 10–12 minutes until lightly golden at the edges.

Matcha Pound Cake
Ingredients:

- 1 cup (225g) unsalted butter, softened
- 1 cup (200g) granulated sugar
- 4 large eggs
- 1 1/2 cups (190g) all-purpose flour
- 2 tablespoons matcha green tea powder
- 1 teaspoon baking powder
- 1/4 teaspoon salt

Instructions:

1. Preheat oven to 350°F (175°C). Grease a loaf pan.
2. Beat butter and sugar until light and fluffy.
3. Add eggs one at a time, beating well.
4. Sift in flour, matcha, baking powder, and salt; fold gently.
5. Pour into the pan and bake for 45–50 minutes until a skewer comes out clean.

Apple Crumble Bars

Ingredients:

For the base and topping:

- 1 1/2 cups (190g) all-purpose flour
- 1/2 cup (100g) granulated sugar
- 1/2 teaspoon baking powder
- 1/2 teaspoon cinnamon
- 1/2 cup (115g) unsalted butter, cold and cubed
- 1 large egg

For the filling:

- 2 cups (240g) peeled and diced apples
- 2 tablespoons granulated sugar
- 1 teaspoon cinnamon

Instructions:

1. Preheat the oven to 350°F (175°C). Grease an 8x8-inch pan.
2. Mix flour, sugar, baking powder, and cinnamon.
3. Cut in butter until crumbly, then mix in the egg.
4. Press half into the pan.
5. Toss apples with sugar and cinnamon, layer over the crust.
6. Sprinkle remaining dough on top.

7. Bake for 35–40 minutes until golden and bubbly.

Raspberry Thumbprint Cookies
Ingredients:

- 1 cup (225g) unsalted butter, softened
- 2/3 cup (135g) granulated sugar
- 2 large egg yolks
- 1 teaspoon vanilla extract
- 2 1/4 cups (280g) all-purpose flour
- 1/2 cup (160g) raspberry jam

Instructions:

1. Preheat the oven to 350°F (175°C). Line a baking sheet.
2. Cream butter and sugar together.
3. Add egg yolks and vanilla, then mix in flour.
4. Roll dough into balls and place on the sheet.
5. Make an indentation in each and fill with a little jam.
6. Bake for 12–15 minutes until lightly golden.

Vanilla Madeleines

Ingredients:

- 2/3 cup (85g) all-purpose flour
- 3/4 teaspoon baking powder
- 2 large eggs
- 1/2 cup (100g) granulated sugar
- 1 teaspoon vanilla extract
- 1/2 cup (115g) unsalted butter, melted and cooled

Instructions:

1. Preheat oven to 375°F (190°C). Grease a madeleine pan.
2. Whisk eggs and sugar until thick and pale.
3. Stir in vanilla.
4. Gently fold in flour and baking powder.
5. Fold in melted butter.
6. Spoon into molds and bake for 8–10 minutes.

Lemon Bars
Ingredients:
For the crust:

- 1 cup (225g) unsalted butter, softened
- 1/2 cup (100g) granulated sugar
- 2 cups (250g) all-purpose flour

For the filling:

- 4 large eggs
- 1 1/2 cups (300g) granulated sugar
- 1/4 cup (30g) all-purpose flour
- 2/3 cup (160ml) freshly squeezed lemon juice

Instructions:

1. Preheat oven to 350°F (175°C). Grease a 9x13-inch pan.
2. Mix crust ingredients, press into the pan, and bake for 15–20 minutes.
3. Whisk filling ingredients together and pour over the hot crust.
4. Bake for another 20–25 minutes.
5. Cool completely and dust with powdered sugar.

Cinnamon Rolls

Ingredients:

For the dough:

- 2 3/4 cups (340g) all-purpose flour
- 1/4 cup (50g) granulated sugar
- 1 teaspoon salt
- 2 1/4 teaspoons instant yeast
- 1/2 cup (120ml) milk, warm
- 1/4 cup (60g) butter, melted
- 1 large egg

For the filling:

- 2/3 cup (135g) brown sugar
- 1 tablespoon cinnamon
- 1/4 cup (60g) butter, softened

Instructions:

1. Mix flour, sugar, salt, and yeast. Add milk, butter, and egg.
2. Knead until smooth, then let rise for 1 hour.
3. Roll into a rectangle, spread with butter, sprinkle with sugar and cinnamon.
4. Roll up, slice, and place in a greased pan.
5. Let rise 30 minutes, then bake at 350°F (175°C) for 20–25 minutes.

Mini Victoria Sponges
Ingredients:

- 1 cup (225g) unsalted butter, softened
- 1 cup (200g) granulated sugar
- 4 large eggs
- 1 teaspoon vanilla extract
- 1 1/2 cups (190g) self-rising flour
- Strawberry jam and whipped cream, for filling
- Powdered sugar, for dusting

Instructions:

1. Preheat oven to 350°F (175°C). Grease a mini cake tin or muffin tin.
2. Cream butter and sugar until fluffy.
3. Add eggs one at a time, then vanilla.
4. Fold in flour gently.
5. Divide between tins and bake for 15–18 minutes.
6. Cool, slice in half, and sandwich with jam and cream. Dust with powdered sugar.

Chocolate Chip Scones

Ingredients:

- 2 cups (250g) all-purpose flour
- 1/4 cup (50g) granulated sugar
- 1 tablespoon baking powder
- 1/2 teaspoon salt
- 1/2 cup (115g) unsalted butter, cold and cubed
- 3/4 cup (130g) chocolate chips
- 2/3 cup (160ml) milk

Instructions:

1. Preheat oven to 400°F (200°C). Line a baking sheet.
2. Mix flour, sugar, baking powder, and salt.
3. Cut in butter until crumbly.
4. Stir in chocolate chips and milk until dough just comes together.
5. Pat into a circle, cut into wedges, and bake for 15–18 minutes.

Peanut Butter Cookies

Ingredients:

- 1/2 cup (115g) unsalted butter, softened
- 1/2 cup (100g) granulated sugar
- 1/2 cup (110g) packed brown sugar
- 1/2 cup (130g) peanut butter
- 1 large egg
- 1 1/4 cups (155g) all-purpose flour
- 3/4 teaspoon baking soda
- 1/2 teaspoon baking powder
- 1/4 teaspoon salt

Instructions:

1. Preheat oven to 350°F (175°C). Line a baking sheet.
2. Cream butter, sugars, and peanut butter.
3. Beat in egg.
4. Stir in flour, baking soda, baking powder, and salt.
5. Roll dough into balls, flatten with a fork.
6. Bake for 10–12 minutes.

Apricot Danish
Ingredients:

- 1 sheet puff pastry, thawed
- 4 tablespoons (60g) cream cheese, softened
- 2 tablespoons powdered sugar
- 1/2 teaspoon vanilla extract
- 8–10 apricot halves (fresh or canned)
- 1 egg, beaten (for egg wash)

Instructions:

1. Preheat oven to 400°F (200°C). Line a baking sheet.
2. Mix cream cheese, powdered sugar, and vanilla.
3. Cut puff pastry into squares.
4. Spoon a little cream cheese mixture into the center and top with an apricot half.
5. Fold corners slightly inward and brush edges with egg wash.
6. Bake for 15–18 minutes until golden.

Savory Puff Pastry Twists

Ingredients:

- 1 sheet puff pastry, thawed
- 1/2 cup (50g) grated parmesan cheese
- 1 teaspoon dried herbs (oregano, thyme, or mixed)
- 1 egg, beaten (for egg wash)

Instructions:

1. Preheat oven to 400°F (200°C). Line a baking sheet.
2. Roll out puff pastry slightly.
3. Sprinkle with cheese and herbs, press lightly.
4. Cut into strips, twist each strip, and lay on the tray.
5. Brush with egg wash.
6. Bake for 12–15 minutes until puffed and golden.

Lemon Poppy Seed Muffins

Ingredients:

- 2 cups (250g) all-purpose flour
- 1 tablespoon poppy seeds
- 1 tablespoon baking powder
- 1/2 teaspoon baking soda
- 1/4 teaspoon salt
- 1/2 cup (115g) unsalted butter, melted
- 3/4 cup (150g) granulated sugar
- 2 large eggs
- 1/2 cup (120ml) milk
- 1/4 cup (60ml) fresh lemon juice
- 1 tablespoon lemon zest

Instructions:

1. Preheat oven to 375°F (190°C). Line a muffin tin.
2. Whisk flour, poppy seeds, baking powder, baking soda, and salt.
3. In another bowl, mix butter, sugar, eggs, milk, lemon juice, and zest.
4. Combine wet and dry ingredients.
5. Fill muffin cups and bake for 18–20 minutes until golden.

Strawberry Shortcake

Ingredients:

For the shortcakes:

- 2 cups (250g) all-purpose flour
- 1/4 cup (50g) granulated sugar
- 1 tablespoon baking powder
- 1/2 teaspoon salt
- 1/2 cup (115g) unsalted butter, cold and cubed
- 2/3 cup (160ml) heavy cream

For the filling:

- 2 cups (300g) sliced strawberries
- 2 tablespoons sugar
- 1 cup (240ml) whipped cream

Instructions:

1. Preheat oven to 400°F (200°C). Line a baking sheet.
2. Mix flour, sugar, baking powder, and salt. Cut in butter.
3. Stir in cream to form a dough.
4. Pat out, cut into rounds, and bake for 12–15 minutes.
5. Toss strawberries with sugar.
6. Split shortcakes, fill with strawberries and whipped cream.

Coconut Macaroons

Ingredients:

- 2 1/2 cups (200g) shredded sweetened coconut
- 2/3 cup (135g) granulated sugar
- 1/4 cup (30g) all-purpose flour
- 1/4 teaspoon salt
- 4 large egg whites
- 1 teaspoon vanilla extract

Instructions:

1. Preheat oven to 325°F (160°C). Line a baking sheet.
2. Mix coconut, sugar, flour, and salt.
3. Stir in egg whites and vanilla.
4. Drop spoonfuls onto the baking sheet.
5. Bake for 20–25 minutes until golden brown.

Mini Cheesecakes
Ingredients:
For the crust:

- 3/4 cup (100g) graham cracker crumbs
- 2 tablespoons granulated sugar
- 3 tablespoons melted butter

For the filling:

- 16 oz (450g) cream cheese, softened
- 1/2 cup (100g) granulated sugar
- 2 large eggs
- 1 teaspoon vanilla extract

Instructions:

1. Preheat oven to 325°F (160°C). Line a muffin tin with liners.
2. Mix crust ingredients and press into liners.
3. Beat cream cheese and sugar until smooth. Add eggs and vanilla.
4. Spoon over crusts and bake for 18–20 minutes.
5. Chill before serving.

Date and Walnut Cake

Ingredients:

- 1 cup (150g) chopped dates
- 1 teaspoon baking soda
- 1 cup (240ml) boiling water
- 1/2 cup (115g) unsalted butter, softened
- 3/4 cup (150g) granulated sugar
- 2 large eggs
- 1 1/2 cups (190g) all-purpose flour
- 1 teaspoon baking powder
- 1/2 teaspoon salt
- 3/4 cup (90g) chopped walnuts

Instructions:

1. Preheat oven to 350°F (175°C). Grease a loaf pan.
2. Pour boiling water over dates and baking soda; set aside.
3. Cream butter and sugar. Beat in eggs.
4. Stir in flour, baking powder, and salt. Add date mixture and walnuts.
5. Bake for 50–55 minutes.

Chocolate Truffles

Ingredients:

- 8 oz (225g) bittersweet chocolate, chopped
- 1/2 cup (120ml) heavy cream
- 1 teaspoon vanilla extract
- Cocoa powder, for coating

Instructions:

1. Heat cream until just simmering, then pour over chocolate.
2. Let sit 2 minutes, then stir until smooth.
3. Stir in vanilla. Chill until firm.
4. Scoop and roll into balls.
5. Roll in cocoa powder.

Tea-Infused Ice Cream
Ingredients:

- 2 cups (480ml) heavy cream
- 1 cup (240ml) whole milk
- 3/4 cup (150g) granulated sugar
- 4 egg yolks
- 2 tablespoons loose-leaf black tea (or tea of choice)

Instructions:

1. Heat milk and cream with tea until just steaming. Steep for 5–10 minutes.
2. Strain out tea.
3. Whisk egg yolks and sugar, then slowly add the warm mixture.
4. Cook gently until thick enough to coat a spoon.
5. Chill completely, then churn in an ice cream maker.

Savory Herb Scones

Ingredients:

- 2 cups (250g) all-purpose flour
- 1 tablespoon baking powder
- 1/2 teaspoon salt
- 1/2 teaspoon pepper
- 1/2 cup (115g) cold unsalted butter, cubed
- 1 tablespoon chopped fresh herbs (such as rosemary, thyme, or chives)
- 2/3 cup (160ml) milk

Instructions:

1. Preheat oven to 400°F (200°C). Line a baking sheet.
2. Mix flour, baking powder, salt, and pepper.
3. Cut in butter until crumbly.
4. Stir in herbs and milk until just combined.
5. Pat out, cut into rounds, and bake for 12–15 minutes.

Orange Loaf Cake

Ingredients:

- 1/2 cup (115g) unsalted butter, softened
- 1 cup (200g) granulated sugar
- 2 large eggs
- 1/2 cup (120ml) fresh orange juice
- 1 tablespoon orange zest
- 1 1/2 cups (190g) all-purpose flour
- 1 1/2 teaspoons baking powder
- 1/4 teaspoon salt

Instructions:

1. Preheat oven to 350°F (175°C). Grease a loaf pan.
2. Cream butter and sugar.
3. Add eggs one at a time. Stir in juice and zest.
4. Fold in flour, baking powder, and salt.
5. Pour into the pan and bake for 45–50 minutes.

Walnut Brownies

Ingredients:

- 1/2 cup (115g) unsalted butter
- 8 oz (225g) bittersweet chocolate, chopped
- 1 cup (200g) granulated sugar
- 2 large eggs
- 1 teaspoon vanilla extract
- 3/4 cup (95g) all-purpose flour
- 1/4 teaspoon salt
- 3/4 cup (90g) chopped walnuts

Instructions:

1. Preheat oven to 350°F (175°C). Grease an 8-inch square pan.
2. Melt butter and chocolate together.
3. Stir in sugar, eggs, and vanilla.
4. Fold in flour, salt, and walnuts.
5. Pour into pan and bake for 25–30 minutes.

Almond Florentines

Ingredients:

- 1/2 cup (100g) granulated sugar
- 1/4 cup (60g) unsalted butter
- 2 tablespoons heavy cream
- 2 tablespoons honey
- 2/3 cup (65g) sliced almonds
- 2 tablespoons all-purpose flour

Instructions:

1. Preheat oven to 350°F (175°C). Line a baking sheet.
2. Heat sugar, butter, cream, and honey until melted.
3. Stir in almonds and flour.
4. Drop spoonfuls onto the sheet, spreading thinly.
5. Bake for 8–10 minutes until golden.

Chai Spiced Cookies

Ingredients:

- 2 cups (250g) all-purpose flour
- 1 teaspoon cinnamon
- 1/2 teaspoon ground ginger
- 1/2 teaspoon cardamom
- 1/4 teaspoon ground cloves
- 1/4 teaspoon ground nutmeg
- 1/2 teaspoon baking soda
- 1/4 teaspoon salt
- 3/4 cup (170g) unsalted butter, softened
- 3/4 cup (150g) granulated sugar
- 1 large egg
- 1 teaspoon vanilla extract

Instructions:

1. Preheat oven to 350°F (175°C). Line a baking sheet.
2. Whisk flour, spices, baking soda, and salt.
3. Cream butter and sugar. Add egg and vanilla.
4. Mix in dry ingredients.
5. Scoop dough onto the sheet and bake for 10–12 minutes.

Brie and Cranberry Tartlets

Ingredients:

- 1 sheet puff pastry, thawed
- 4 oz (115g) Brie cheese, cut into small pieces
- 1/3 cup (80g) cranberry sauce
- 1 egg, beaten (for egg wash)

Instructions:

1. Preheat oven to 400°F (200°C). Grease a mini muffin tin.
2. Cut pastry into squares and press into tins.
3. Place a piece of Brie and a little cranberry sauce into each.
4. Brush edges with egg wash.
5. Bake for 12–15 minutes until puffed and golden.

Honey and Oat Bars

Ingredients:

- 2 1/2 cups (200g) rolled oats
- 1/2 cup (115g) unsalted butter
- 1/2 cup (120ml) honey
- 1/3 cup (65g) brown sugar
- 1/2 teaspoon cinnamon

Instructions:

1. Preheat oven to 350°F (175°C). Grease an 8-inch square pan.
2. Melt butter, honey, and sugar together.
3. Stir in oats and cinnamon.
4. Press mixture into the pan.
5. Bake for 20–25 minutes until golden.

Pumpkin Muffins

Ingredients:

- 1 3/4 cups (220g) all-purpose flour
- 1 teaspoon baking soda
- 1/2 teaspoon salt
- 1 teaspoon cinnamon
- 1/2 teaspoon nutmeg
- 1/2 teaspoon ginger
- 1/4 teaspoon cloves
- 1 cup (200g) granulated sugar
- 1/2 cup (120ml) vegetable oil
- 2 large eggs
- 1 cup (240g) pumpkin purée

Instructions:

1. Preheat oven to 375°F (190°C). Line a muffin tin.
2. Whisk flour, baking soda, salt, and spices.
3. In another bowl, beat sugar, oil, and eggs. Stir in pumpkin.
4. Add dry ingredients and mix gently.
5. Fill muffin cups and bake for 18–20 minutes.

Rhubarb Crumble
Ingredients:
For the filling:

- 4 cups (500g) chopped rhubarb
- 1/2 cup (100g) granulated sugar
- 1 tablespoon flour

For the topping:

- 1 cup (125g) all-purpose flour
- 1/2 cup (100g) brown sugar
- 1/2 cup (115g) unsalted butter, cubed

Instructions:

1. Preheat oven to 375°F (190°C). Butter a baking dish.
2. Toss rhubarb with sugar and flour; spread in the dish.
3. Mix topping ingredients until crumbly.
4. Sprinkle over rhubarb.
5. Bake for 35–40 minutes until golden.

Salted Caramel Brownies
Ingredients:
For the brownies:

- 1/2 cup (115g) unsalted butter
- 8 oz (225g) bittersweet chocolate, chopped
- 1 cup (200g) granulated sugar
- 2 large eggs
- 3/4 cup (95g) all-purpose flour
- 1/4 teaspoon salt

For the caramel:

- 1/2 cup (100g) granulated sugar
- 2 tablespoons water
- 3 tablespoons heavy cream
- 1 tablespoon unsalted butter
- Pinch of sea salt

Instructions:

1. Preheat oven to 350°F (175°C). Grease an 8-inch square pan.
2. Melt butter and chocolate. Stir in sugar and eggs. Fold in flour and salt.
3. Pour into pan.

4. Make caramel: heat sugar and water until amber, then stir in cream, butter, and salt.

5. Drizzle caramel over brownie batter and swirl.

6. Bake for 25–30 minutes.

www.ingramcontent.com/pod-product-compliance
Lightning Source LLC
LaVergne TN
LVHW061950070526
838199LV00060B/4049